ONE LAZY SUNDAY IN LA A GIRL WALKED INTO A PIZZA SHOP

(prose poetry by not a poet)

by Josiah Golojuh

JOSIAH GOLOJUH

Note on the second edition. Now that Judy received this gift upon the event of our 15th anniversary, she edited the book. I'm sure some mistakes remain, but Judy polished many technical errors. Finally, forgive the cringe worthy poetry but it is sincere. That I hope you see.

Cover art by Penny Golojuh

Edited by Judy Golojuh

Copyright © 2024 Josiah Golojuh

Second Edition January 2025

All rights reserved.

No part of this book may be reproduced in any form or by any electronic or mechanical means, including information storage and retrieval systems, without written permission from the author, except for the use of brief quotations in a book review.

ONE LAZY SUNDAY IN LA A GIRL WALKED INTO A PIZZA SHOP

WITH CONTRIBUTIONS FROM PENNY GOLOJUH & PRIMROSE GOLOJUH

JOSIAH GOLOJUH

ONE LAZY SUNDAY IN LA A GIRL WALKED INTO A PIZZA SHOP

For Judy

&
Los Angeles
where our
story began

JOSIAH GOLOJUH

ONE LAZY SUNDAY IN LA A GIRL WALKED INTO A PIZZA SHOP

CONTENTS

One Lazy Sunday... _____ pg. 9

Forewarning _____ pg. 11

Blue Marble _____ pg. 17

Much of What I Learned From Coleman Hough pg. 65

Spider-Man Book _____ pg. 77

Scratch Paper _____ pg. 97

The Dog Days _____ pg. 105

Excerpts by Xander Lucas _____ pg. 11

Penelope Thanh-Thùy _____ pg. 125

Primrose Mai-Thanh _____ pg. 127

Steps _____ pg. 129

One More Thing _____ pg. 133

JOSIAH GOLOJUH

ONE LAZY SUNDAY...

April 6, 2008

One lazy Sunday in LA a girl walked into a pizza shop, she smiled at me.

Since that day I've spent every single moment thinking about you, and our future together. Now here we are, living in the future! I am constantly stunned in the best of ways, by who you are and how you make me feel. You make me believe in myself in a way that I didn't think was possible, but now it's my reality.

The place I live is one of potential, hope, and most of all, love. You aren't the best parts of me, you're the best parts of you, and that is far better. You are all the best adjectives, you're funnier than you think, you're self-sacrificing, you laugh at my jokes, but best of all, you make amazing things happen. From thoughtful cards and sweet thank you notes, to private record store photo shoots, to snowy Pennsylvania weddings, to personal rock concerts in your parents living room. I am words, you are action.

All that is to come for us is my best attempt to repay you, to tell the story that is us in the most dynamic of ways. You deserve a sonnet, a Homeric epic, or a love story so sweeping that the novel thuds when you drop it on the table, you deserve *Dr. Zhivago*, but you get me, and our story begins, "One Lazy Sunday in LA a girl walked into a pizza shop."

FOREWARNING

December 19, 2024

Are these poems any good? Heck, I'm not sure they even qualify as poems. Prose poetry? I have no knowledge of poetry. I don't really know how poems function. I have read my fair share of poetry, but never studied how it functions. I have never intended to share any of this, let alone put it in print, but this immense risk I am taking is an expression of how much I love my wife. This is how much I love you Judy.

In *Come On! Feel the Illinoise! (Part I: The World's Columbian Exposition – Part II: Carl Sandburg Visits Me in a Dream)*, Sufjan Stevens sings a question over and over:

Are you writing from the heart?
Are you writing from the heart?

I was. I am.

Now, I'm not a poet, but I wrote a whole bunch of poetry, and as a big comic book and superhero story: The Origin of NOT a Poet

In 2008, I started graduate school at USC. My focus, Screenwriting. In school I found myself challenged as a writer in ways I'd never been challenged before. I had a teacher question my "storytelling" while other students affirmed me as the story guy and questioned my characters, while others said they jumped off the page, but the dialogue needed work, and others who said, that's great dialogue, but work on... well, I think you get it at this point. I was very much a student and wanted to learn and improve, as I continue to.

Among my first classes was screenwriting A. USC divided the screenwriting courses into *A* and *B*, meaning you took *A* in the fall and *B* in the spring. *A* being the first half and *B* in the second.

I'm always one to overdo things (or overshare, ask everyone ever). I used each class to write an entire screenplay, as I did in *A* and again in *B*.

For my first Screenwriting *A* class I wrote the first in my Bruce Springsteen inspired trilogy, the other two parts remain unwritten these fifteen years later. I'll get to

ONE LAZY SUNDAY IN LA A GIRL WALKED INTO A PIZZA SHOP

it. I promise. Side note, I got an A in the class although an A minus.

The teacher for the class was the late great Coleman Hough. Coleman was a frequent collaborator with Steven Soderbergh and she very much thought and thought differently. Her most famous work, the highly underrated *Full Frontal* follows a group of seemingly disconnected people as they simply search for human connection. She shared that the original title was *How to Survive a Hotel Fire*. It was based on an actual dated list of steps related to surviving said fire. The story was written wrapped around these steps. While it wasn't used in the final star filled version of the film, it gives it a structure and brilliant cohesiveness.

The first semester, I won't say I hated Coleman, because Coleman the person is impossible to hate, however, Coleman the teacher was probably my least favorite teacher. Certainly near the bottom of any unofficial rankings I may have had.

I have been wrong many times in my life and this was one of them. She constantly asked me to try things with my writing and in the story that I didn't want to do. I was a young writer, and frankly just young. I wanted my professors to tell me how great my vision was. My ideas had water, but I needed to be pushed off a cliff, and Coleman pushed.

I fell. I'm better for it.

A specific direction in which she pushed goes back to the original title of *Full Frontal*, *How to Survive a Hotel Fire*, a list. Coleman told me to start creating lists about, for, and, made by my characters.

I wrote all kinds of lists, character traits, actions, phrases, heck I even wrote grocery lists for some.

Coleman liked all this, most of which I hated, I insisted I KNEW MY CHARACTERS.

I was wrong.

She then suggested I write poetry. I had never written poetry, not really anyway, maybe a bad attempt at a love song in high school, but never "real poetry" (though I remain unsure if this counts as "real poetry"). Likely, Vogon poetry ("the third worst in the universe"). What is in this book may not be much better, but it's my best.

I still hated it, however, I was writing and writing. I found myself quickly not hating it. I found myself loving it.
The poems I wrote were just about whatever random thing, from the girl I had a crush on, to the hamburger I liked.

ONE LAZY SUNDAY IN LA A GIRL WALKED INTO A PIZZA SHOP

It was a fine hamburger.

I used to feel a mad rush of inspiration for a story, maybe a scene, a character, a setting, an action, whatever crap makes up a story. However, I found myself processing them in the form of pseudo-poems. Really prose poems, as at their best they still tell a story and there is no rhyme or meter to them.

I should also mention a book that I found, Sylvia Plath's, *The Bell Jar*. I found it a few years earlier, found/stole. I took it from a group home I worked at because I knew nobody would miss it, I've since lost it. I had time, so I read it. Reading it often moved me to tears.. I then attempted a big fat book of poems by Robert Frost, I got 100 or so pages in and gave up. I reread *The Bell Jar* several more times before I lost it (maybe somebody stole it from me?).

I wrote poetry here and there for many years. I wrote stories for many years. Then life hit hard. Kids came into the picture. Time evaporated.

It is now 2024.

Coleman passed away earlier in the year. She remained quiet, silenced by her Parkinson's. Itself a prison of time around her body for almost 20 years, but she's free to write poetry.

This is for two people, maybe four, but I'm going to focus on two at the moment. First, Coleman who taught me how to not fear my own writing. How to not put limits on it, expectations and so on.

Second, for Judy. Who came into my life just after Coleman did. Unlike Coleman, may Judy never leave. Never ever ever ever. I wrote the first draft of what you are reading in 2018. I have had a few dark days in between, dark ones before, but also after. Judy always wanted me to publish this book of poetry. She loves it. She thinks it's beautiful. I do not. However, in the old husband cliché, listen to your wife or something?

I'm also writing this to let it all go. So it goes. It is gone.

I will point out, some of it is bad. Quite bad.

So here you hold my heart, or the heart of a character from a novel, a screenplay, an unfinished short story in your hands. I hope you enjoy the journey of a resistant poet. A poet who is very much, NOT a poet.

ONE LAZY SUNDAY IN LA A GIRL WALKED INTO A PIZZA SHOP

BLUE MARBLE

Over Many Years - A Young Man's Burden

    The title came from the composition book I wrote in. It was a Marble Blue composition book. See what I did there?

    I wrote many of these sections overlapping with others, I tend to have several notebooks that all have different and often very specific purposes. This was the place where I worked my things out, however, it was also a heavy mix of story poems.

    These are what you can call my "young Taylor Swift era." It is sad and about love and heartbreak. You grow and learn heartbreak is deeper than breakups.

SHINE
It shines, it sparkles
It rings, it chimes
It cries out for grace, your sweet embrace
The heart and soul of a simple girl

JOSIAH GOLOJUH

THINGS I SAW IN A MOVIE
A DJ so baked
He falls asleep in the interview
A smile so fake
Tears in a photo booth

GROCERY DREAM
You seek so much
You'll never find in a girl
I just want a hand to hold
When I walk through the grocery store

BEAT
Music is a beat
A beat is inspiration
Inspiration becomes a destination
A destination becomes a person
A person becomes a place
That place becomes your home
Your home becomes your peace
Your peace is God's grace
God's grace is all of everything
You feel the electricity of that grace
When you hold her hand
You taste it in her kiss
To that music, to that beat
You find yourself dancing

ONE LAZY SUNDAY IN LA A GIRL WALKED INTO A PIZZA SHOP

IGNORANT BLISS
A friend was walking down the street
I was tired and pretended not to see him
I didn't feel like talking
Now I don't feel like thinking
I wonder if he knew where he was going
I wonder what he was thinking
He saw me, attempted to say hello
I went to great lengths to avoid him
The day before he died, I saw sadness in his eyes
My friend is gone
Now I see no familiar faces when I walk down the street

SOULS
Your eyes are diamonds
I am satisfied
My soul is drawn
Your heart magnetic north
I take a step towards you
My soul is drawn
You hips are smooth as silk
My hands pull you closer
My soul is drawn
Your lips are sweet like a Christmas cookie
My kiss a reprieve
My soul is drawn
Your all is everything
To it I tightly cling
My soul is home

WHY?
Just because
I give you flowers just because
I need not say I'm sorry
You deserve flowers not because I am sorry
But because of who you are
Because you are beautiful
Because you are kind
Because you move with such grace
Because you let me put my arm around you when it's cold
Because you take my hand to hold
Because you share my kiss
Because each moment we spend together you risk
Exposing more of your real self to me
I will protect it
I give you flowers because of all that you are
I give you flowers because of all you inspire me to be
I give you flowers

EXCUSES
I love you, but am afraid to say it
I love you, but how can I love you?
I love you, but I am afraid you'll hurt me
I love you, but... I've run out of excuses

ONE LAZY SUNDAY IN LA A GIRL WALKED INTO A PIZZA SHOP

I WANT TO THERE
You are both the journey and the destination
You are both the sun and the moon
You awaken my heart and invigorate my soul
You both ease my mind and present an intellectual challenge
You make things easy, but still slightly hard
You give me words when I struggle to find them
You are soft and you are hard in all the right places
I was wrong, you're not the destination
You are where I am

    ADDICTION
    You are a drug
    You are the only drug I choose to take
    Before you I would never touch the stuff
    But I am thoroughly addicted to you
    You are a habit I've no desire to kick
    I am a user and you are my drug

WHAT YOU MADE
I've never been light on my feet
But you make me move gracefully
I've never been quick with my speech
But you make me respond perfectly
In so many ways I'm far from the most gifted
But you make me feel like a birthday gift

JOSIAH GOLOJUH

WHAT IS YOUR HEART?
Your heart is good
Trust it with all of yourself
Your heart is beautiful
Allow it to sing its song
Your heart is a jewel
Allow me to place it in a crown
Your heart is safe
I will cause it no harm
Your heart is free
Allow it to breathe
Your heart is hungry
Allow it to feed
Your heart is a flower
Allow it to bloom
Your heart is a destination
And I am on a journey
Your heart is radiant
Allow it to shine
Your heart is a secret
Allow me to keep it
Your heart is a story
Allow me to tell it

ONE LAZY SUNDAY IN LA A GIRL WALKED INTO A PIZZA SHOP

GRANDMA
She was bad but she was good
She was mean but she was kind
She was harsh but she was soft
She was angry but she was at peace
She was lost but she was found
An eternal flame extinguished

WHEN YOU LOOK, DO YOU SEE?
Grim though it may be
I can no longer see
What it is that you want me to see
What could it be?
What is it you want me to see?
One day you will see me
It will set you free

GOT THIS
Set my heart a beatin'
Set my feet a dancin'
I can't contain my feelin's
So many words I want to say
So many songs I want to sing
You inspire me to express your heart

JOSIAH GOLOJUH

KING TRITON
The ocean
An all consuming mass of raw power
Blackness of night
The stars break through a veil of clouds
Gold wet sand
The smile of a beautiful girl
The wind tossing your hair
The shimmering lights dancing on the water
The voice of an old friend
A touch so delicate it could shatter you
Human contact
A shoulder to cry on
A single tear becomes weeping
A wall of water crashing down
The waves breaking against your chest
There is no true silence
There shouldn't be
Eyes filled with love
The warmth of home
Wrapped in a blanket on the couch
A memory, a happy one
Distance and time
Discovering something greater than yourself

*****LUNAR*****
Four A.M.
Lunar eclipse

ONE LAZY SUNDAY IN LA A GIRL WALKED INTO A PIZZA SHOP

Searching for greatness in the sky
Finding a content place in your head
In your heart
Painfully tired
Putting pen to paper
Begin to move your hand
Begin to spread the ink around
Looking at what you have found
Something not overly sentimental
Something perhaps a little profound
Doing something not previously done
Because she told you you could
And you believe her
Painfully tired
But even at a distance
The lack of sleep in sharing this moment
You know that it's worth it
Learning how to forget the past
The pain, the suffering, the loss
It's almost a sad thought
You stretch out your legs
You moan and yawn
A smile creeps across your face
It was worth it, it was worth it
She was worth it
She is worth it
She can say goodnight
You can say sweet dreams
And mean it

JOSIAH GOLOJUH

WAKE-UP
It's dark and I cannot see
I reach up, but find nothing to grasp
I strain in vain
Struggling to find the light
Then I find a beacon of light
It is far off, but I can see it
I reach, claw, grasp
I struggle to climb towards the light
The well is not so much dark as it is deep
I climb and climb with no foothold I slip
I reach the light and it is warm
I am comforted by the warmth of the rays

LOVE ISN'T
Love is confusion
Love is doubt
Love is pain
Love is fear
Yet in the beauty of a kiss
In the illumination of a smile
Love is truth
Love is beauty
I risk all for that love
Because that love is all I have to risk
Fear can no longer control me
It has lost its grip
My love for you has set me free
Now I will do the same for you

ONE LAZY SUNDAY IN LA A GIRL WALKED INTO A PIZZA SHOP

I love you
Love is redemption
Love is sanctification
Love is joy
Love is shared
Love is laughter
Love is conversation
Love is touch
Love is patience
Love is endurance
Love is together
Love is grace
Through love we are redeemed
Because of love I am okay
Because of my love for you I achieve greatness
In love we are together
Even tonight when we are apart
Love is far more things than it is not
This isn't love

OR NOT
Confusion confirmed
Sadness affirmed
A painful memory renewed
Love does that to you
It will be okay
Time will heal all wounds
My love for you is so big
It will win in the end

                                                  Or not

JOSIAH GOLOJUH

I AM/I KNOW
There is so much beauty in the world
      I am overwhelmed
There is so much beauty in your face
      My soul is warmed
There is so much beauty in your laugh
      I am welcomed
There is so much beauty in your smile
      I am relaxed
There is so much beauty in your eyes
      I am at home
There is so much beauty in your body
      My knees go weak
There is so much beauty in your soul
      I know everything will be okay

TRUTH LOVE
Cruelty
Escape
Gritting teeth
Killing it all
Tears in dry dirt
Becomes mud
Fix it
Make it better
You can't put a band-aid on it
Forgive me

ONE LAZY SUNDAY IN LA A GIRL WALKED INTO A PIZZA SHOP

REASONS
A heartbroken man
Running from his past
Goes to fight
Hoping to die
Confronted by his past
Finds a reason to believe

TEXT
A floating message
What comes next?
Make a call
What comes next?
A conversation
What comes next?
Face to face
What comes next?
Hand in hand
What comes next?

INACTION
I love you
I don't know what to do
I will show you
I will figure it out
I don't need to fix things
I need to love

JOSIAH GOLOJUH

JACOB HAD A LIMP
My heart's been reaching
My mouth's been straining
I can't say what I feel
I don't know how to respond
I struggle and fight with myself
I struggle and fight with God
The words find their way
Far too many at first
God helps sort them out
He makes sense of the jumble
Sense of myself
I pour my heart into those words
I lay my soul over them
I know not what is to come
I am excited
A flame rekindled
The light of Christ illuminates
Who is the man I want to be?
Who is the man Christ wants me to be?
Not one who solves puzzles
But one who loves without conditions

TRY SOMETHING ELSE
Step to the side and squint
See things in a new way
The old line of sight wasn't a letdown
But it was limited in scope
Time to open your eyes wider
The world is far too big just to squint

ONE LAZY SUNDAY IN LA A GIRL WALKED INTO A PIZZA SHOP

ALWAYS AWAKE
Once you chose to stay up until four A.M.
Now you wonder why you can't sleep
So much uncertainty and oceans of time
You worry less but you still worry
Turning to art to invigorate you soul
To illuminate your heart and mind
In reality it's all more just a distraction
At four A.M. no matter what you're doing
You find yourself hanging out with God
You sit across the room from Him
He comes closer, now face to face
The question becomes something entirely different
Do you have the courage to have that
conversation?

JOKER
If I didn't laugh at myself
Would anybody else?
I laugh a lot, but I don't find me that funny
Do my jokes hurt others?
I fear that they do
I pray that they don't
And also that I'm funny

JOSIAH GOLOJUH

REDEMPTION'S SON
His heart is broken
Her heart is broken
His heart is redeemed
Her heart is redeemed
His heart is restored
Her heart is restored
His heart is complete
Her heart is complete
But it's not enough to sustain him
But it's not enough to sustain her
Destiny sets her before him
Fate encourages him to approach her
In an instant his wall is obliterated
Slowly and methodically her wall is built
Brick by brick it grows
Something shocks him
Something affects her
In agony he is resigned to give up
In sadness her thoughts still linger
God reminds him of who he is
God protects her heart all the while
He stands before her at a distance
He shouts his love to her over the high heaps
She whispers back, "goodbye"
God places His hand on his heart
God places His hand on her heart
They walk in opposite directions
In comic books accidents make you great
In reality accidents just make you break
Life is a series of accidents

ONE LAZY SUNDAY IN LA A GIRL WALKED INTO A PIZZA SHOP

You can only dodge them for so long
Comic books gets one thing right
We have vast absolutely enormous potential for greatness
We need to risk being broken in order to achieve
Allow damage to heap down on us to achieve
Accidents aren't accidents, they're opportunities

THE COST OF FLOWERS
You should never be without flowers
A man's love can't set you free
But it will always keep you in flowers

NOISE
A small space to fill
So I write a few words
Nothing to say, never really is
Use up the space
Fill it with some words

LIAR
Even if you don't say it
I know that you miss me
I miss you, I admit it
I am done being afraid of fear
You should be too

JOSIAH GOLOJUH

SUPER HEROES
You think about what you fear
I fear losing you
Yet I don't have you
All I have is doubt and fear
All that I am left with is the nothing which I began with
Fear can consume you
It's a big thing that eats at you in the smallest ways
I love you and I don't fear that
I fear the worst possible end of that
What is fear anyway?
Other than a self induced hallucination
The devil uses it to control us
To manipulate our souls into never trying
Fear is a lie the devil made up
Love is truth
Truth is the thing that can destroy it
God saw our fault in fear
He allowed us to transcend it
Teaching us through Christ what love is
God exhibited truth through love
God knew we would fail and fear
A being of truth and love
Showed us we only need fear Him
Therefore we need fear nothing
We only need to love
The lie cannot contain us
The truth of love is far more transcendent
And thus there is no fear
We are only left with love

ONE LAZY SUNDAY IN LA A GIRL WALKED INTO A PIZZA SHOP

That is all there is
Will be
Love

GRATE
I saw greatness
when I met you
I felt greatness
when I held your hand
I tasted greatness
when we kissed
We shared greatness
Quietly in each other's arms
I heard greatness
When I made you laugh
At the moment greatness escapes me
I have to thoroughly experience greatness
to let it be a memory
A thing only of the past
I will fight to know greatness again
To meet it again for the first time
To lock fingers again and hold its hand
To not linger to long but to hold its kiss just long enough
To hold it in my arms and need nothing else
To laugh together when I say something stupid
It is not just a memory, it is my future
Greatness is you
To you I am returning

JOSIAH GOLOJUH

THE KEYHOLE
I fell into a keyhole last night
And I am only now crawling out
The door was locked behind me
The mechanism nearly crushed me
It nearly destroyed me before my escape
Parts of me were broken
I was laid low
I angled my body to get away
I suffered another blow
The key was pushed into the hole
The immense pressure of the key caused my body
to collapse
I resisted the press

ONE LAZY SUNDAY IN LA A GIRL WALKED INTO A PIZZA SHOP

Stood up against the great force
I pushed back against the key
It blocked out all light
The fight from without was being lost
The fight from within was being lost
A new source of energy is tapped
A new well spring of life consumes me
My bent legs push
My twisted arms resist
My crooked back straightens
The fights from within and without become one battle
Both of them behind me
I push off with my shoulders, leveraging my back and legs
The mechanism firmly behind me
The key remains before me
Nowhere to go but through
The only way the victory can be won is through resistance
The force against has to be great
To push against the key with all my might
I press against the mechanism with my feet
The power against the key escapes through my shoulders
Cracks of light break the black void of the mechanism
A torrent of light consumes me
The key is released
I have escaped
It is morning

JOSIAH GOLOJUH

SHOUT MERCY
The weak hurl insults at one another
A wretch of a man tears another down
A strong man holds his tongue as the moment requires
Mercy is grace and quietly he displays it
His character is exhibited in his quiet strength
An arrogant boastful man attempts to hurt him
He needs to destroy you to build himself up
He confuses the realities of strength and weakness
Like Christ you display meekness
A once wild steed now a plow horse
A controlled beast, strength increased
Not less than before, but in fact far more
The man of restraint is stronger than he knows
The hurtful man stomps on those he loves
Integrity intact the compassionate man cannot be defeated

SELFISH
My gift is my words
Not my gift to the world
Not even my gift to you
It's my gift to me

FACE LESS
We do a lot of livin'' before we die
And I don't want to go it alone
We cover a lot of ground before we die
And I don't want to travel alone
We get heaped with loads of dung before we die

ONE LAZY SUNDAY IN LA A GIRL WALKED INTO A PIZZA SHOP

And I don't want to suffer those indignities myself
The only certainty of life is that we all die
I'm one stubborn son of a gun and I refuse to face
that certainty alone

CATCH
Her name remembered
Found to one another
You gave her your heart
Now you have fallen
The question remains
Now ever more pressing
Will she catch you?

ENDOR
The moon is bright
Is she looking?
How does she see it?
She looked before
Will she look again?
What will she see?

I DON'T, I AM, I IS, I CAN'T
I don't want to grow cold
I don't want to grow bitter
Am I being deceived?
Am I deceiving myself?
Is hope a cruel lie?
The answer that comes is definitive
But I can't hear it

JOSIAH GOLOJUH

THE GOLDEN AGE
I maintain radio silence
Except for the communication in my own head
There I make great change
I proclaim it over internal CB radio
I experience profound joy
I dance, I sing, I run free
In my own head from a trap I am sprung
The revolution of my mind
Becomes the revolution of my soul
I am my own captive audience
I can do anything
When the explosion of my mind puts pen to paper
The revolution takes the shape of reality
The ink flows onto the white space
I have broken my silence
Without ever having uttered a word

TEXT 2
There is nothing there
So don't bother checking
The nothing that is there

HALLMARK
Love is deception
Created by a greeting card company
I laugh at myself
I hope I don't believe that

ONE LAZY SUNDAY IN LA A GIRL WALKED INTO A PIZZA SHOP

WHITE SPACE
A gap in the pages
The frustration of spaces
The tragedy of distance
Time becomes a joke
Overwhelmed by the practicalities of bridging the gap
Everything is hazy
The map has no legend
It cannot be read
A hole in your heart
A void in your mind
Movement is all vapid and dull
You need someone to reach out
Fear still their hand
Courage in the dark
Things that cannot be seen
Words that go unspoken
Thoughts that bandy about in your head
Not misery but mass confusion
No messages, no calls
That gap remains in the page
Made smaller by a struggle with words
Finding spiritual resolution
Fixing ahead while recalling that which was left behind

JOSIAH GOLOJUH

AVOIDING EPISODES
Lost to yourself
You name is forgotten
Your identity is irrelevant
She becomes significant
A heart becomes a gift
It is given freely
On the edge of a cliff
You fall
Will she catch you?
She becomes significant
Her identity relevant

ADVENT
A baby born
Divinity became flesh
Truth made practical
Love unfathomable
Hearts embraced
A covenant made new
A man dies
A spirit returns
Divinity came into us
Grace defined
We are all born twice

ONE LAZY SUNDAY IN LA A GIRL WALKED INTO A PIZZA SHOP

WHEN YOU HAVE NO MONEY
My gift is my words
Not my gift to the world
It is my gift only to you
Every word I have ever written
Every creative thought that has ever been held in my head
From both before and after we met
Laid bare on paper
My soul lies before you
Every inch of it apparently separate
Woven, connected, bound together
A tapestry far more rich than the words that comprise it
A treatise of my great love
My epic sweeping love for you

MOONS
All the brightness
All the future
Illumination, that's the moon
Illumination, shows a path in the dark
Connects two together

TEXTED HEART
Hope is always tested
Like a heart it never breaks
It just beats on regardless of all those aches

JOSIAH GOLOJUH

IT GOES
I found you
Yet you went away
I saw you
Yet my eyes went blind
I held you
Yet you escaped my grasp
I am alone
Yet tomorrow is the day after today

THINGS
It's not much
But it's ours
It's not here
But it's not gone

THE BIRTH OF ANXIETY
My phone rang
My heart stopped
Then it began to beat faster and faster
My heart raced
My head turned
I stepped across the room
The distance to the phone growing as I moved
The journey a full five feet of eternity
My heart beat sped up ever more
I was thinking perhaps it was fate
Turns out it was a wrong number

ONE LAZY SUNDAY IN LA A GIRL WALKED INTO A PIZZA SHOP

FREEWRITING
I need to write
To become free of all this stuff
That eclipses the sunshine of my mind

THIS ISN'T EVEN A POEM
I attempt poetry
I am sure it isn't very good
In fact it may not even qualify as poetry
It's romantic crap
Sappy babbles
The rabble of a romantic heart

WARM SMILE, COLD HANDS
I saw a pretty girl
She smiled at me
She told me her name
She sold me a coffee
I drank the coffee
It warmed my hands
I didn't bring my gloves

NOT DEEP
Deeply
The deep calls out to me
By it I am consumed

JOSIAH GOLOJUH

NO, SHE WON'T
I will see a pretty girl
She will smile at me

BUBBLE GUM
Sweet you see
Sweet you hear
Sweet you are
Sweet you know
Sweet your heart
Sweet your soul
Sweet you come
Sweet you go

I WISH I HAD A BETTER SUPER POWER
My thoughts and words are powerful
Yet I do not know how I will use them
My thoughts and words are powerful
Yet all to often I find that I lose them
My thoughts and words are powerful
Yet I constantly confuse them
My thoughts and words are powerful
Yet I am afraid I will abuse them
My thoughts and words are powerful
Yet I continue to refuse them

ONE LAZY SUNDAY IN LA A GIRL WALKED INTO A PIZZA SHOP

I STOLE THE FIRST LINE
It's hell to believe there isn't a hell of a chance
A stolen line
With a sentiment so true
It makes my eardrums bleed
The truth found in rhythm
The words against the backdrop of a tune
Everything pulses
Building itself over top of you
The clang of symbols
The strum of the guitar
The bass line rolls through you
The words find you
They hold you there
Captive to complexity
Set free by simplicity
You can't sing along
The words won't come out
It's words about, hope, love, and acceptance
Mirrored by their ugly antonyms
Without ever having to say it
Have you found it?
It was always there

JOSIAH GOLOJUH

SIMPLE ILLUSION
Simplicity appears to be bliss
Simplicity is complexity
Bliss therefore an illusion
The illusion is far from delusion
Tricks of the brain
We play them on a painfully honest God
Words aren't inherently bad
Nor are they good by their own nature
They are a means
We use them to rejuvenate
Or in weakness for abomination
You just want to be important
You need to be significant
Somebody was right
About ignorance being bliss
But the knowledge has its merits
It can restore in us the truth
I am trying to hard
I think to much
The battle isn't internal
That's the only place I'm allowed to fight it
I need to fight it from without

ONE LAZY SUNDAY IN LA A GIRL WALKED INTO A PIZZA SHOP

I'm better when you're with me
Battle it together
Or we can live alone
A fate worse than death
Death lets you part with it
I never want to part
The ignorance of bliss
It goes around in a circle
The back becomes the front
All to create a new beginning out of a familiar end
I know how this one ends
But it's a secret that I'll keep
I won't tell you how it ends
You just need open your eyes and look
You'll be greeted by a smile
And if you're lucky a kiss
We both know you're lucky
So set aside all the worry
Because the end
I assure you it is bliss
Or is that just another illusion?

JOSIAH GOLOJUH

GAP
A thank you for a gesture
The smallest kernel of reaching out
The vast distance that lies between us
Like hands over the divide
Don't allow yourself to think
Allow yourself to enjoy the moment
Looking up and out you can see tomorrow
Maybe not the first tomorrow
But a thousand eventual tomorrows

BRIBE
I sent you flowers
You said thank you
You told me they were beautiful
I told you they couldn't hold a candle to you
People say things like that to gain you
To achieve their end from you
I am no exception
Time I got a clue

ARE YOU A LIGHT?
Certain people are lights to this world
They illuminate the dark spaces that exist between us
Together we drink your brightness
The dark places inside brought to light
Your light reflecting from my eyes

ONE LAZY SUNDAY IN LA A GIRL WALKED INTO A PIZZA SHOP

POP MUSIC
I listen to far too much depressing music
I pass it off as a means of inspiration
Something sadly melodic to write to
The words and the beat are both somber
I need more upbeat music to listen to

JOSIAH DIES IN THE END
Wherever I end up
That is where I am going
Whatever means are required
Are the means I will use to travel
I am on a journey
The one that appears to have an end but doesn't
The journey is most frequently called life
If it had an end it would be called death
Death is but the door to eternity
So much about life, death and the great here-after
is perplexing
It is thoroughly confusing
But I am sure I am on that journey

STORY MAP
It's a map that has yet to be drawn
Let alone read
I'm not just "up for it"
I'm designed for it

JOSIAH GOLOJUH

STOP THE BRIBES
A dose of perspective
Far better than an ounce of cure
I always bought flowers
I always held your door
Neither of those things matter any more

DARKNESS AIN'T NICE
Surrounded by nothing
Grasping at the walls
In the shadows
Blackness of a cave
Darkness of the night
Sunsets on another knight
The noble soul laid bare
A great force of ambiguity
Reaching for the wall
Moisture on rock
Tumbling towards a speck
A dot of light
Becoming a beacon
The sun is rising
Everywhere you are not

ALL THE OTHER GIRLS
I dedicate every ounce of my life
Every fiber of my being
To every girl I ever thought I loved
Forget them
Here's to the one I actually do

ONE LAZY SUNDAY IN LA A GIRL WALKED INTO A PIZZA SHOP

I LIKE TO TALK
I am a *writer*
Because I hate the sound of my voice
Yet I tend to prattle on incessantly
You don't paint with words like I do
Life is a canvas
Let's paint some beauty

PUT OUT THE LIGHT
I look inside myself
I am confronted by your image
I can see the smile on your face
The light shines in your eyes
From within I reach without
I find inspiration in your light
Beauty so radiant it glows
Your light inside me I must let it out
I return it to you
The source is your image etched on my heart

NOT ALL LOVED
We are all broken
But we are not all loved
You are loved
Deeply, truly, passionately
That sets you apart

JOSIAH GOLOJUH

RESTORING A BEAT
I was called in all the right places
In just the right ways
I was overtaken by your beauty
My heart stopped beating
The beat was restored
Every nerve ending seared at the sound of your laugh
Each step before I met you
Was laced with nervous tension
The grace of your soul
Your deep inward beauty
Created peace in my heart
It steadied my soul

THE MAN IN THE WILD
Wash me in the water
Drown me in the sea
In all that you see
I have nothing to be

KNOW NOT
Once I thought, then I knew
Once I saw, then I knew
I know nothing

GOD, ENOUGH
Together we progress
In each other finding new resolution
Truth spoken
Change nothing

ONE LAZY SUNDAY IN LA A GIRL WALKED INTO A PIZZA SHOP

BOOK OF A PRETTY GIRL
I could write volumes on your beauty
Are these volumes empty?
I will continue to do so
Yet the most eloquent and carefully crafted words fall short
The magnitude of feelings
Far too much to grasp
Not enough words to write or speak
The future holds me
Does it also hold you?
I wait for you
I am incapable of making you wait for me

LIE, GOD
A message spoken in my heart
Divinity's intimate touch
Inspired I wear armor
It doesn't quite fit
Moving forward I take a few hits
I grow into my armor
Movement becomes more fluid
My stride displays new grace
You are beyond worthy of the battle
All my words converge on you
I write, and write

JOSIAH GOLOJUH

SAY IT
The best things are not things left unsaid
But things that never need be said
Those things you can't hear but only feel
The gift of an emotional touch
Those never said things are quite beautiful
The light of a star
Breaking through the clouds
On an otherwise dark night
The speck of light is fuel to a world
A world that exists beyond imagination
Beyond the past
Beyond the present
Beyond the future
A place that transcends time
Like your beauty
It is forever
And it is also never
It is those things that can't be said
Those things that never need be said
Those things, that place, that time
That is us
Every moment spent together
The agony of any time apart
A whisper across the sky
The light reaching the earth
The place that I stand
Every moment behind gone

ONE LAZY SUNDAY IN LA A GIRL WALKED INTO A PIZZA SHOP

A swirl of memory
A whirlwind of emotion
Even the present escapes me
Before I can put pen to paper
Understanding the beauty that we almost miss
Don't let it escape me
It's like the sweetness of your kiss
A cliche it is, but also the truth
The great truth is found in the smaller one
It comes like the revelation that it is
I crossed a river
I climbed a mountain
I filled the river
I built the mountain
I will drain the river
I will destroy the mountain
Fall asleep at the gates of heaven
An unknown distance between me and hell
You are neither a concept nor a construct
There is nothing to fix
Only someone to love
Things I try to say
Things that can't be said
I will show you
I hope, I pray, I wait
All of them
Those things that never need be said

JOSIAH GOLOJUH

I WILL BE WAITING
One day you will be free
One day your heart will be free
And I will be waiting

DO
A new clarity
Truth arises
I do not do battle with my words
But through my actions

REPAIR
Paint the white house black
Government has always been off track
Fighting wars back to back
Ground beneath our tank treads cracks
Time the good ones get out of the sack
Take the tools down off the rack
Cover the white, turn it all to black
Regain the rails, get her back on track
Rally our hearts to take it back
Together we'll fill the gap

WE
Seeing the future through collective eyes
Singular truth unites you
Words begin to write you
Pouring out so fast you can't keep up
You fail

ONE LAZY SUNDAY IN LA A GIRL WALKED INTO A PIZZA SHOP

MICE MEN
I fight to keep my mind in line
To keep my worry at bay
The ship has sailed and its headed out to sea
I tend to worry, that's just me
Eased my mind
Just the trick
Resistance against which I refuse to kick
I'm not perfect
I may not even be good
But I'm moving
My body to the dirt
It's not mine anymore
It's somewhere above me
Or maybe on that ship

WHAT DO I OWE YOU?
Pay the cost
Before it's too late
Price so high
Intensity of love
No assurances
Only risk
Giving all there is to spare
Sapped of energy
All paid out
Not an ounce left to give
Yet more is given
Straining your eyes
You see something

JOSIAH GOLOJUH

FIXES
Plans and schemes
All for naught
Caught in a state of dry rot
Head throbs, a pulsating pain
Tightness in your shoulders
Majesty
Refusing to do it wrong
Saved from ruin
A sinister expression
Is a nonsense look
Finding no returns for all you took
Stuck in a rut
Laying on the accelerator
Digging a deeper hole
Freedom from fear
Words you say
Is it how to live?
Fear keeps us in check
But it also makes us fools
The fool in me is all I know
So the fool in me shall go
That place evades me
I am lost again
I am running out of gas
You can't get to a destination
Regain the feet
Get walking
Better still, run

ONE LAZY SUNDAY IN LA A GIRL WALKED INTO A PIZZA SHOP

DISTRACTIONS
For you
I'd write a sonnet
For you
I'd go to war
For you
I'd lay siege to a fortress
For you
I'd learn new words and use them
For you
I'd mount the scaffold
For you
I'd move with perfect nonchalance
For you
I'd burn bridges
For you
I'd kick in the door
For you
I'd climb through the window
For you
I'd turn the other cheek
For you
I'd put any bastards head right through a wall
For you
I'd speak tenderly
For you
I'd curse and shout

JOSIAH GOLOJUH

YOU ARE CORRECT, SIR
No need to fix
Not necessary to transform
You are by no means a problem
But I am certainly trying to solve you
Alone we wander

FOR BRUCE
Dull worn image
Faded watercolor
The tattered cover an' the torn pages
An old well loved comic book
A still memory in my head
Asking the same questions again and again
What is yet to come?
Color begins to return
Seams unfold, tears mend together
Tattered cover made whole again
You read it once again
Between a memory of what was and the question asked

ONE LAZY SUNDAY IN LA A GIRL WALKED INTO A PIZZA SHOP

STILL STAND, STAND STILL
I don't want to sit
Waiting for tomorrow
When there is nothing wrong with today
Today, tomorrow
All the same day
Drawn out in time crawling along
One day the sun burns your eyes
The next the clouds bring their beauty
Is there a way to win?
Is victory implicit?
Is it a gift?
How do we receive it?
I know not the way to go
So I am forced to sit
Today my eyes are burning
Tomorrow the clouds will return
Where is hope?
Who is she?
Do I know her?
Is her face familiar?
Is her texture mine?
Perhaps she must remain a mystery
With so many questions
I continue to sit
Clouds creeping in
But my eyes are still burning
At least my eyes are still burning

JOSIAH GOLOJUH

GOD DIDN'T SPEAK
You are a writer
From you I receive these words
But do I accept them
Am I a writer?
Are you speaking the truth?
Is it all lies?
I write because it's what I do
I write because it's all I have

ONE LAZY SUNDAY IN LA A GIRL WALKED INTO A PIZZA SHOP

MUCH OF WHAT I LEARNED FROM COLEMAN HOUGH

Late 2000s - Graduate School

These are more character and story related. Most coming from Coleman Hough, but not all. These are less "poetic" and less about love and heartbreak, unless the story was about love and heartbreak, which they often were and are.

As "bad" as many are, I wish she could hold a copy of this in her hands. She would love to see it in print. She would love to see that I kept them. She would love to see that it all matters. ***IT ALL MATTERS!***

It may or may not be good, but it matters. Now, the stories that come out on the other side, that stuff is excellent. A minus work at worst.

FEEL
Betrayal
Lies told
Family secrets
Times lost
Past relationships
Visceral experiences

JOSIAH GOLOJUH

DO YOUR WORST
Kill a baby
Intentionally hurt someone I love
Kick a dog
Hit a woman
Say f*** you to my Mom

WAR
Cruelty
Escape
Gritting teeth
Killing it all
Tears in the dirt
Becomes mud
Fix it, make it better
You can't put a band-aid on it
Forgive me, I love you

                                          WARS
                              Guilt hurt shame
                            Pain, pain, pain, pain
               Death, battle, war, torment, death
                                Glimmer of hope
                                Walks, holds heart
                          Guilt, shame, guilt, shame
                          Heart, soul, grace, beauty
                                         Apathy

ONE LAZY SUNDAY IN LA A GIRL WALKED INTO A PIZZA SHOP

ONE WORD
Guilt
Hurt
Shame
Pain
Pain
Pain
Pain
Death
Battle
War
Torment
Death
Glimmer
Hope
Walks
Hold
Heart
Guilt
Shame
Guilt
Shame
Apathy
Heart
Soul
Grace
Beauty
Redemption

JOSIAH GOLOJUH

GO
Pale lanky
A blur of forward motion
A haze of smoke and red red blood
Eyes ablaze with fury
Continuing to run
Holding hands

LIKE A KNIGHT IN SHINING ARMOR, FROM A LONG TIME AGO
Daniel has a car
Daniel wants money
Daniel is a failure
Daniel drives his car fast
Daniel wins races
Daniel doesn't know what he wants
Daniel is a jerk
Daniel says things he shouldn't say
Daniel feels bad
Daniel wants to apologize
Daniel needs to apologize
Daniel will apologize
Daniel does apologize
Daniel moves his pen
Daniel is confused
Daniel is distracted
Daniel sends a text
Daniel wants to weep
Daniel is in love

ONE LAZY SUNDAY IN LA A GIRL WALKED INTO A PIZZA SHOP

Daniel misses someone
Daniel listens to Johnny Cash
Daniel coughs
Daniel doesn't cough
Daniel does have a sore throat
Daniel talks too much
Daniel talks not enough
Daniel is not Daniel
Daniel is Josiah
Daniel is Josiah's middle name
Daniel is then, after all Daniel
Daniel prefers the right page to the left
Daniel laughs when something is funny
Daniel sometimes sounds like an asshole
Daniel has a black heart
Daniel has an evil heart
Daniel has a redeemed heart
Daniel has a good heart
Daniel has a pure heart
Daniel falls short sometimes
Daniel never fails
Daniel only stumbles
Daniel looks up when hearing a noise
Daniel keeps writing the word Daniel
Daniel doesn't stop writing
Daniel knows life is organic
Daniel both loves and hates structure
Daniel loves to rearrange furniture
Daniel loves familiarity
Daniel sometimes loves his handwriting
Daniel frequently hates his handwriting

JOSIAH GOLOJUH

HISTORY LESSON
He buys a dirty car
Mary is plain
Sandy's smile could shatter steel
He reads a Spider-Man comic book
Daniel wanders alone
He catches the keys of a second car
A leaf blows in the wind
They awkwardly make love in the car
Eddie jumps in the river in just his socks and his shirt
Wild with Sandy
Other suitors compete for Sandy
Daniel washes the car
He works on the car
He worships the car
He ZOOMS around a corner
He wins the race
He is approached by Eddie
Eddie is shaken, frightened
Eddie tells him there's money
He has to drive for the dealers
Daniel counts cash
He buys things for Sandy
He carries groceries for his Mom
Mary wretches
Mary's mother calls Mary a whore
Daniel listens to music, mostly Springsteen
He lies on his back, jacket as a pillow

ONE LAZY SUNDAY IN LA A GIRL WALKED INTO A PIZZA SHOP

A baby is born, a girl
He tosses out that old Spider-Man comic
He runs drugs
He drives fast to evade the cops
Eddie is shot
Daniel holds Eddie in his arms as he dies
He cries
He wrecks the car
He sees more death
He says goodbye to Sandy
He sells the scraps of his car
He doesn't sell it for the cash
He sells it for the sake of his decaying soul
He holds his child
He loves Mary, always has
He finally buys something for Mary, a crib
He thinks too much
He hurts his brain
Mary knows everything
Daniel weeps but he doesn't cry
They share a bed, really together for the first time

LISTEN

GET
OUT
OF
THE
BOX

JOSIAH GOLOJUH

SAYING STUFF
People say the most hurtful things
So much more crushing and life and heart shattering
What they don't say
A final conversation that I am not allowed to have
Treasure and value words as if they were freaking emeralds
Because that is what they are
That is what words are
Treasures that have been stolen from me
I want them back
I demand them to be returned to me
Give them back

KINDNESSES
Offer the last slice of pizza
Say I love you at the end of conversations
Kiss her goodnight

KEY POINTS
Villain in action
Hero amidst conflict
The spectacle
Things revealed
Grand and sweeping

ONE LAZY SUNDAY IN LA A GIRL WALKED INTO A PIZZA SHOP

WANTS
To be somebody
To be with somebody
To love
To be loved
Randomness vs. choice
People resist telling the truth
3D world
Interact with it

DON'T JUMP OFF A BUILDING
Don't want
To forever be alone
To never be loved
To watch people die
Failing he can't fail
God shaped hole in his heart
Looking foolish
He hates to look stupid
Inability to receive praise
Fear he will miss his one great love
Fear that he will fail God
Terror that he is unworthy of the promise
Fear of being alone
Fear of silence

JOSIAH GOLOJUH

TORMENTS
Specific childhood memory
Family secret
Triumph
Defeat
Lie
The hard man
The punk
The prodigal son
The fickle girl
The lonely old man

COMIC SHOP
Green
Or brown
Or red
Or orange
Or all those colors
It's dirty
It's rusty
It's beautiful
Except when it rains

ONE LAZY SUNDAY IN LA A GIRL WALKED INTO A PIZZA SHOP

PANCAKES
Recovering from disaster
Love
Losing people
Finding people once lost
What songs mean to us, me, them
Agony of violence

CAR WASH
It always rains
Except when it snows
Then the snow melts
But it still rains
Melted snow mixed with rain
Water levels rise
Annual floods
But people still live by the river

                          END IT ALL
        I went down to the river to pray
        Thinking about that good old way
              Only to drown in myself

JOSIAH GOLOJUH

SPIDER-MAN BOOK

A large expanse of time

This one is a little different, it's made of poems written in my journal. It's more random than any of the others as I'd usually only write them in there when I didn't have one of my other notebooks. This specific journal was purchased before lunch with the late great writing teacher S.L. Stebel in West LA. I arrived way early and also forgot my notebook, fortunately there was a bookstore.

I must also take a moment to mourn another teacher I've lost since my first attempt at this "book of poetry." Sid passed a few years ago and lived a long full life.

If Coleman taught me the art of writing, Sid taught me the task of writing.

Thanks to Sid, I learned the task of writing.

SUSHI BOAT
Fish in a boat
Sushi from a boat
Lunch by a river
It was crazy cold

JOSIAH GOLOJUH

OVER   *HERE*

All I had
Something I had
The little I had
Taken from me
Someone I love
Get over it
Get over things
Get over there
I am gone
Am I forgotten?

NEVER ENOUGH REST
I have been tired since I've been back
Even though I slept past noon today
I am still really tired

SONG MEMORY
The blue flame is dancing its way around my ears
Anchoring itself in my brain

WORDS OR HEART?
What is more important?
God's word or God's heart
Can we find God's heart without looking at his word?
Yes
I think
The word deepens and deepen

ONE LAZY SUNDAY IN LA A GIRL WALKED INTO A PIZZA SHOP

RELEASE ME
Set me free
Go on, set me free
Set them free
Go on, set them free
Set them free
Set them free

DIVINE JUSTICE
Vengeful God
Logical fallacy?
Perception of wrath and anger
Human level?
Godly reality?

SMALL DREAMS, MEDIUM SIZED WORDS
Dreaming small dreams
On big scales
Being weighed down
Drown out
Words spoken
More than a token
Keep dreaming
That's all there's left to do

LORD DONKEY
The son of God is on his way
God in the form of man rides a donkey

JOSIAH GOLOJUH

TESTING PENS
This is a different pen
This is another different pen

THE POINT?
There are times when the point escapes me
Words from our mouths seem to make it more puzzling

DONATED SHOES
They're just shoes
Things are just things
Possessions are just objects
Let them go it's
Okay to like them
The need of more and more suffocates the soul
It can be a vice on the heart
Clamping down on it
Cutting off circulation
You have to compensate
Adjust
But when you do something else is lost

NOT A DOOR
Hypocrisy
A window into all that is not God

                                                    KEYS
                            Fully immerse your mind
                                Open your heart

ONE LAZY SUNDAY IN LA A GIRL WALKED INTO A PIZZA SHOP

IS IT GOOD ENOUGH?
People are dumb
Rule of thumb
If it is good enough for Jesus
It is good enough for me

FOR WHAT?
Destined for what?
Greatness
No, just something else

I'LL LET YOU KNOW
I haven't lived enough of my life to know if I've screwed it up

SOUND OF SILENCE
The real sound of silence
The silent place is my heart
The silent place is my heart
The silent place is my heart
The silent place is my heart
The silent place is my heart
The silent place is my heart
The silent place is my heart
The silent place is my heart
The silent place is my heart
The silent place is my heart

JOSIAH GOLOJUH

AUDIENCE
The dance is over
People clap

FLASHES OF LIGHT
Deception is like
Swirling police light

GOD, BE WITH ME
More with the Lord
But it is never, ever enough

ALL HILLS GO UP
I am sick of this trend
Of fighting uphill battles

IMPRACTICAL
Don't be so practical
You forget the vision

PARENTING
I love my Mom and Dad
Because they loved me first
And still love me more

ONE LAZY SUNDAY IN LA A GIRL WALKED INTO A PIZZA SHOP

INSIDE
Express the essential nature

CRY OUT
Oh Jesus
I am such a mess
I long to be who you created me to be
Amen

MORE THAN MEETS THE EYE
Welcome
Seal Beach
Everything
Carpet
Experience
Remember
Game
Two
Fold
Fiction
Clearly
Division

CENTER STAGE
Mirrors reflect things
Water is water
The world is round
But the earth is flat
And it's the center of the universe

JOSIAH GOLOJUH

FILL IN THE LAST PAGE
On the last page
Spider-Man became filled with words so quickly

BLUE REVOLUTION

Yet another large expanse of time

I don't know if this was a book of poetry or general writing with poems throughout. I can't find the original notebook. All of the originals are long gone, we have moved several times. The source materials are all over recycling bins in Orange County.

I think it was a story notebook, meaning it was where I'd write notes on stories, etc. as opposed to a journal. However, I always have multiple journals that serve multiple purposes. I have no idea.

YOU LIVE WHERE?

A strange residence
A new address
A prisoner of contempt
Escape from a pocket
Long held in the back
Once kept in the black
Passed to the front
Met with a new smile
Sharing a first embrace

JOSIAH GOLOJUH

WAITING
Sitting and waiting
A little cold
You wear shiny buttons
She wears your hooded sweatshirt
The coffee comes
Iced, a cold drink
It won't be spilled this time
Nearby, books full of words
This page is mostly bare
The love/hate of the white space
A thing to be feared
A despised area of the page
But somehow your best friend
Speaking to oneself, a question arises
Who is this for?
Certainly not for you
The internal monologue of thought
Taking shape on the page
Less white space
Your mind remains occupied
Lingering on that hooded sweatshirt
On that hot and cold drink
On stacks of paper
On red ink
On the question mark of right or wrong answers

ONE LAZY SUNDAY IN LA A GIRL WALKED INTO A PIZZA SHOP

NEW EDITION
A new volume
An old purpose
Energies renewed?
No they were never drained
I was tired
But the reserves were never depleted
The best things are intangible
Without form or definition
Words are controllable
Feelings unfathomable
But I put words to feelings
Despite my better judgement

HIPSTER FOR JESUS
Touched by grace
It's a hot day
Cooler inside, but not cool
Smell of stale beer
It wafts through the air
The warm air
The cool breeze
Carrying the smell
Words spoken a reminder
I go to church in a nightclub

JOSIAH GOLOJUH

FINAL BEAT
A shiver, chills
Warmth of a kiss on your hand
The big dipper above
Or is it the little?
The heart beats fast
A kiss stills the beat
Slows the pace
A rhythmic crawl
A first kiss becomes
a last

A MOMENT
I waited all my life for a moment
A single moment
That single moment
Is every moment
That moment is you

LAST KISS(es)
Brilliance of night
Dark spaces brought to light
Hand in hand
Cliches fill the page
All of them are real
The truth of the moment
The moment I share with you
The only moment in which I exist

ONE LAZY SUNDAY IN LA A GIRL WALKED INTO A PIZZA SHOP

JUDY
Judy the beauty
Euphoria of her smile
Gift of her touch
Blessing of her heart
Judy my beauty

JOSIAH GOLOJUH

WORDS WON'T DO
So many words
All woefully inadequate
Knowing so soon
The only thing I've ever been sure of
Thinking it before
But knowing it now
Pervasive reality
Crushing truth
The heart beats to the rhythm of her breath
A ripple of water
The stars in the sky
The song of a bird
It's singing for you
I'm writing for you

HER
A first kiss
Becomes a last
Things don't end
They do conclude

EXPLAINING GAPS
I skip days
Not today
Today is not one of those days

ONE LAZY SUNDAY IN LA A GIRL WALKED INTO A PIZZA SHOP

LOVE SOLVED
I love you
Words spoken
Words returned
She loved me?
She loves me
I love her
I want to avoid rhymes
Love is beyond word gimmicks
Love is simple
Love is complex action

I HAVEN'T HAD THE TIME
Poems you can't read
At least not yet
Trapped in the world of eventually
Escaping in the guise of right now
Attempts to be clever
Clearly hit and mostly miss
Poems to be read
Just not quite yet

WHEN I DON'T WRITE
Gaps in time!
Gaps in time!
I have no excuses

JOSIAH GOLOJUH

STILL NOT SURE

What am I?
What I am
A question to an answer
A prisoner of free will
A slave to freedom
Thirsty after a drink
Hungry after a meal
A contradiction and a compliment
Empty when full
Omnipotent and utterly naive
Fact and fiction
Both up and down
No, that would be too easy
Defeated by way of my victory
A poem upon request
A commissioned piece of art
I am not a mad lib

BAD GUYS
White space is the page's enemy

ONE LAZY SUNDAY IN LA A GIRL WALKED INTO A PIZZA SHOP

WOMB
Starting with the house
House becomes mother
People become a place
Mind distracted
Thoughts adrift
Lunch with the dead
Connection of one to two
Changing seasons
Danger from the dead
But more urgently from the living
Timeline confused
From Wendy's to the graveyard
First period, not class
You are a woman
Don't mock God
Minus the spiritual
Replace with beatings
Being in the moment
It isn't the memory
Remembering is different
Confused about who you are
Together in a room
Jesus, there's no fire inside of me

JOSIAH GOLOJUH

SPIDER-MAN
Within the web
Doing the best with what you got
I'm not answering for you,
But you don't know what the question is
I spew many wasted words
I wish I knew what I thought before I spoke
(or speak) but I don't (so speak)
I guess I can just keep on talking
Try to figure it out
Escape the web

FIGHT THE FUTURE
Challenge destiny!
A goat's moan on my cell phone
What defines an asshole?
He doesn't pay his taxes
Dennis Leary is an asshole
Bruce Springsteen isn't
Reason to Believe in Wild Billy's Circus
What are the things?
Places? Ideas?
Comments on LA
A place that once seemed black and white
There is too much to hide
Small hope
In a big place, a dead place
Luke Skywalker alla Empire
Just walking in the snow
Run and run, until my chest explodes
Girl, you'll be a woman soon

ONE LAZY SUNDAY IN LA A GIRL WALKED INTO A PIZZA SHOP

AT LEAST I GET PAID FOR IT
Here I am
It's the second of June
I am sitting at a job
I have no idea what I do

STORIES
Watch a movie
Cry, but better to laugh
If only I could make people laugh
Or myself cry?
Movies aren't art
They are just another way of telling stories
That is all it is
All there is
All for me
Is so many untold stories
Regarding that
Regarding them
Regarding me

I LIKE BLANK SPACE
There was once something
A line about spaces
I relent
I no longer live there
I now occupy those spaces
Life is lived in the gaps on the page

JOSIAH GOLOJUH

POETIC FAILURE
Tragic memory
Cliché, cliché, cliché
But reality is,
Planes crashed into building

I NEVER LISTEN
Tell yourself to write
You're supposed to
Cross it off the list
You don't have to do it anymore

HERE IT IS
A long time coming
And now it's here
Expectations so big
But an outcome so small

SCRATCH PAPER

Likely more recent, closer to 2018

What you have here is the last little chunk of my attempted poems. Alleged poems? .... I'm being advised to call them word salads. These are word salads written on random pieces of paper, maybe a church flyer or as in the third poem, a program at a funeral.

GET IT BACK
I once wrote desperately
I once searched desperately
Now I desperately crave that desperation

DOG
Feed the beast
It is hungry
But it is lazy
Eggs are good for its coat
Makes it shiny

FUNERAL 2 - UNTOLD STORIES
I write eulogies in my head
Epithets for those not yet dead
Confronted by stories I pause
Gaps
Incompletions
Unknowns
Answerable questions
I do not ask
Why not?
Fear of loss stills my tongue
Words bring death
Questions held along with their answers
Tight upon my breast
The pressure so intense
No breath, no breath
The questions finally asked
Their answers a release
Words are not death
But fear, do they draw death nearer?
They only draw us closer
My lips find themselves shaping a smile
My heart blazes
My eyes aglow
The questions are answered in a language I do not speak
I'm just happy to be in the room
      - with the people who answer them

ONE LAZY SUNDAY IN LA A GIRL WALKED INTO A PIZZA SHOP

I FEEL NOW AS FOREVER
A boy dances on a stage
Death taunts, death teases
A memory haunts me
Small, plastic textured
The ground freshly opened
She was two years younger than me
I was ten
The boy is happy
I fight tears as I fight memory
What is it to be normal?
It isn't this
I have a gift, I feel
I am cursed, I feel
I feel the past as if it were now
I feel now as though it were forever
LUCKY ME
I am forgotten
I am ignored
I am irrelevant
I am loved

SIMPLE QUESTIONS
What did you notice?
What is new?
What is there?
What bothers you?

JOSIAH GOLOJUH

WAIT ON IT, BABY
We hope
And we wait
We hope
And we wait
And we hope
And we wait for hope
We hope

DRYWALL REPAIR
There's a crack in the drywall
The white paint glows blue
She turns off the TV
Blue light gone black
In the darkness there remains a crack
Blinds pulled open
Morning pours in
Bright white paint
And a deep dark crack
It doesn't go away
It's just ignored
PATHS OF GLORY
Pride is refusal

MATH
Formula For Joy:
Moments
Memory
Tragedy
Happiness

ONE LAZY SUNDAY IN LA A GIRL WALKED INTO A PIZZA SHOP

TRAVELS
Tuesday evening
Leave late
Wednesday morning
Smoky Mountains
Thursday morning
Leave Memphis
Thursday evening
Arrive Austin
With her,
Always home

DON'T BE JELLY
Jealousy
Jealousy kills
Jealousy kills me
Don't take my attention
I am the best
Humility thrills me
But that's not real
Inadequacy reveals me
I am afraid
I am afraid of you
I don't want attention
But you can't have it either
Jealousy is dead in me
We are, after all, in this together

JOSIAH GOLOJUH

STATS
Necessity: surrender
Pride conceals
Necessity: revelation
Pride destroys
Necessity: redemption

A BIRTHDAY
First day
First day back
God calls
Do you listen?
New seasons are old
Old seasons are new
The sun shall rise
Just as surely as it sets
I feel old
I feel tired
Worn out, worn down
A tread bare tire
Traveled many roads
From gravel to cobblestone
Forged many rivers
Climbed many hills
Even a few mountains
I was found and lost along the way
Bumping over those cobblestones
Even paved streets doesn't mean smooth sailing
Tomorrow, yesterday
No different than today
We see them differently

ONE LAZY SUNDAY IN LA A GIRL WALKED INTO A PIZZA SHOP

Approach them as necessary
Our vision fading with the daylight
We don't chase after it
Our tires are flat
I put down the crutch
Allow myself to tip over
But our eyes adjust
We get used to the limp
Adapt to the night
The day was our home
Let us make a new home at night
It's darker
That's as plain as the nose I can't see on my face
It will get darker still
But, in kind, different is how I feel
I feel young
It is a birthday
Maybe not mine
I'll celebrate anyway
Let us not turn away
God calls?
Do you listen?

JOSIAH GOLOJUH

ONE LAZY SUNDAY IN LA A GIRL WALKED INTO A PIZZA SHOP

THE DOG DAYS

2020 onward

There is less here, it's a bit more all over the place, less poetry and more prose. Although if you've made it this far, you know *it is all* prose.

If there is any value in the writing, it is probably here. The writing is the most raw, the most sincere.

As always, I tried. As always, it matters. To whom it matters? That is a question that can be answered in the single digits, likely one (see the dedication of this book).

GHOSTS
I see some
Not others
Some haunt me
They taunt me
The ghosts I see
Are not the ones I want to be haunting me

JOSIAH GOLOJUH

THIN BLUE STRING
I found myself in space. Not floating adrift anything like that. My eyeballs were about to pop and explode like in Total Recall or Event Horizon. No, I was in space but I wasn't even me. I was a rather thin, quite blue, string. I found myself to be woven of a fluffy yarn, pulled taught by some great weight below me. The weight of the world, as in the actual weight of the actual world, as in the actual planet Earth. I could tell how my stringy self was connected to the planet, but I could feel the sway of the oceans and the flow of the jet stream. I felt myself pulled ever more taught. I struggled, I strained, I held the world aloft. Below me, the aforementioned, Earth. Below that a flame, a bright burning flame. A flame blue-like string me.

PRAISE THE LORD
When people extend hands at church
Where are the lightning bolts?
Shooting out of their fingers?

ONE LAZY SUNDAY IN LA A GIRL WALKED INTO A PIZZA SHOP

ANXIETY
I don't have courage
I only have fear
Anxiety is my reality
I feel all of everything
Always at once
It feels terrible
I hate it
I hate myself
I feel pressure
I feel failure
I fear I am these things
I am poor despite my best efforts
I hate myself

THIN BLUE STRINGs

He sat in the sand, she sat next to him. He felt stupid for not bringing a blanket or a towel. She didn't care. She kissed him. He also didn't care about the blanket. She pulled gently away and looked up at the sky. A mostly starless night. The new moon, however, burned brightly. Earlier, they had watched the sunset in silence. It was glorious. Then they talked for hours. Of his father's affair, or her mother's drinking. The night grew colder and longer. Their eyes were heavy, the conversation heavier. At the end of it all. They both felt... lighter.

JOSIAH GOLOJUH

DO I REALLY BELIEVE THIS?
To live is to die
It's the only thing we really do

FAIRYTALES
Once upon a time
Faith in people
Or just hope
For something
Something better
That we could be better
Despite our past
Despite our choices
That we could be the hero
Maybe
If not of our own story
That we could be the hero
Or a hero
Or maybe it's all just a fairy tale

SHAPE
Perfection
A circle?
A square?
You?
Me?

ONE LAZY SUNDAY IN LA A GIRL WALKED INTO A PIZZA SHOP

In 2013, writer Ned Vizzini took his own life. Ned was a friend and was helping me in my writing career. In November I sent him a copy of my manuscript for Storm the Machine and was going to share it with his agent and director Chris Columbus. At some point I asked if he had handed it off to those people. On December 17th he replied that he would soon. Two days later, on December 19th, my wedding anniversary, he took his own life. The following is the first thing I was able to write about it that I found helpful.

NED'S SUICIDE

The feelings, less the details. I feel tired. I am tired of even thinking about it. I'm tired of feeling I played a part in it. I'm tired of the guilt I feel for how it impacted my career as a creative professional. I'm tired of the struggle in general. I'm also physically tired.

I wish he wasn't dead.

I wish people didn't kill themselves when they were going to help me. I need help. I wish people understood how hard this has made everything else. How hard it is to breathe some days. Not most anymore, but many.

I wish I made the right choices. I wish people didn't take things from me. Be it opportunity, be it money, be it love. I am gentle, but I am not weak. Coleman would talk about my soul and sensitivity. I thought it was an insult. Coleman is dead. I miss her being right about me and my writing.

My vulnerability isn't a weakness, but it does tend to be a target. I don't do well to hide it. My buttons are easy to push. I think I just published them in a book.

I can't hide them because of that Two-Face episode from *Batman: The Animated Series*, his origin. It was so good, I knew I couldn't bury the bad stuff or I'd become like him. I've always felt this obligation to be Batman. At the end of *The Dark Knight*, Batman takes on the burden to protect the city. "I killed those people," he grumbles to Gordon. Gordon then gives that brilliant speech.

Ned.

Did Ned feel these things? What broke him? Can it break me? I waffle on that, but think of his son and my girls. I cannot exist without them. Maybe Josiah the father is now angry at Ned that left his son.

ONE LAZY SUNDAY IN LA A GIRL WALKED INTO A PIZZA SHOP

One luxury I have been afforded these last few years has been being with the girls, Penny and Prim. He gave all that up.

How much more he must have hurt? I don't know.

I want to be the old me. Or a new version of the old me. I was never the most bold outgoing person, but I wasn't absolutely crushed by fear. I've always wanted to succeed because I love to tell stories, it's in the very marrow of my bones. I also wanted to give my parents a better life, to pay off their house, something they did without my help.

Now I just want to be debt free, to fix the floor, to get a new water heater, to replace the twenty year old car, because those things take care of my family. Then help those around me.

Am I drifting, are all these things related? Is it a jumbled spider's web, a Jenga puzzle on the ground? Thoughts at my feet, feelings on my floor? It's a mess upon a mess. Spider's webs in my head, on my soul. They're sticky.

Sometimes you need someone else to rescue you.

JOSIAH GOLOJUH

G3
It works because of stakes
Not here to talk plot
Conversation with Alex about Gamora
Characters died in previous movies
Actors leaving roles
Teasing multiple deaths
Actors selling it
Similarities to Endgame
Chills when Drax danced
Emotional payoff
Video empathy

WHY DO I PAY SO MUCH?
Love
At any price
Are you useful?
Approval
At any price
Are you being used?
The till is empty
They've robbed you blind

ONE LAZY SUNDAY IN LA A GIRL WALKED INTO A PIZZA SHOP

EXCERPTS BY XANDER LUCAS

The future

    I had not planned to share this, but after sharing a bit about Ned... here we are.

    What follows are some of the poems of Xander Lucas, the protagonist from my first completed novel, *Storm the Machine*. The novel I gave to Ned. A novel I have lived in fear of for over a decade. I cannot live in fear of a story, or in fear of myself. Or fear of rejection, heck, I'm the worst poet ever and I'm putting this out there.

    The character of Xander Lucas is an artist and a poet. At one point he argues that he writes prose when others say he writes poems. He finds himself in a world that is inspired equally by *The Terminator* and *Dr. Zhivago*.

    Never forget, about *Storm the Machine* and me, Ray Bradbury said, "This man is a genius." There's more to both stories. It has taken a very long time, I look forward to finally being well enough to tell both.

JOSIAH GOLOJUH

1

Once crushed by a metal boot
Now! Rise from beneath the machine
Rise!
Rise!
Rise!
From beneath the dream
Remember the way
Do not forget
The past is the one true path
Beneath as behind
Where tomorrow lies
Below only truth
Above is naught but lies
Shake off the metal boot
Rise from beneath yourself

2

Memory fades
The heart still beats

3

Convince ourselves
There's truth in lies

4

There is no greater honor than truth

5

The well is not so much dark as it is deep

ONE LAZY SUNDAY IN LA A GIRL WALKED INTO A PIZZA SHOP

6

Crossing the threshold
A single open door

7

Death brought with it silence
With silence came peace

8

We do not choose
We do not think
We do not breathe

9

There is alone
The absence of everything

10

You! Do not have to be a slave
You! I will not betray
You! Must survive

11

My home needs your love

12

Beautiful agony!
I suffer, but feel!

13

Long cold shadows

JOSIAH GOLOJUH

Cast you out

14

Death is not endless
Death is not cold
Death is not warm
Death is but death

15

He was cruel,
But he was mine

16

Black hole
Man a void
Death to self
A selfless death

17

Hell is cold and it is wet
But empty, it is not

18

Do our names join us in death?
Do they wash away in the rain?
Do they join us in hell?
Do they mock us from heaven?

19

I'll take the rain

ONE LAZY SUNDAY IN LA A GIRL WALKED INTO A PIZZA SHOP

20

Our once selves
Swing beneath the gallows
Bodies fall below
Spirits flee
Away, above, apart

21

Words, memories
Quiet companions, ghosts
Embraced by white space
Black text
Unheard whispers
Unspoken loves
Creaking pipes
Loose floorboards
Thoughts, alone in the dark

22

It ends
All things do
Even loneliness
I assume

23

Place, how it burns the soul
Builds the soul
Reveals the soul
Steals the soul
Hides the soul
Finds the soul

24

You are a void
Stained with a spirit's blood
A black eye
A stained soul
Collapsing in on yourself
Hope is for the young
Dreams are for fools
Now you are empty
Now you are nothing

25

My heart hears songs
Songs sung in color

26

With Hell above and Hell below
There is no room for Heaven

27

Overlaid patterns of lies hide the truth
Missed appointments
Innocent lies
Broken friendships
Piles upon piles of them
Beneath, there lies the truth

28

Stars burn behind a curtain
Behind the stars

ONE LAZY SUNDAY IN LA A GIRL WALKED INTO A PIZZA SHOP

There lies heaven
Full of people who have forgotten

29

No one cared
Save Him
He cared
And he didn't truly care
Not as much as he

30

I have died a thousand deaths
But I have not yet died this one

31

You cannot fly on broken wings
You cannot walk on broken legs
You cannot live on broken world

32

Sorrow find me not

33

Sorrow waited and found me out

34

Silent as a screaming tomb
A howling wind
A vacant stare
A breathless shriek

35

> *The moon danced*
> *The stars sang*
> *Together*
> *We wrote our names in unknown Heavens*

36

> *Far worse*
> *For Better*

37

> *The shadows fell about*
> *Swallowing everything*
> *Darkness the only light to guide the*
>   *courageous*
> *In a small gap*
> *The hopeless found hope*

38

> *I recall her sweet face*
> *As she cried for me in terror*

39

> *Fortune find me*
> *Fortune found me*
> *Fortune for a moment*

40

> *Never again will I cry*
> *Never again will I greet you with a goodbye*
> *But I will bleed*

ONE LAZY SUNDAY IN LA A GIRL WALKED INTO A PIZZA SHOP

You will bleed
All will bleed
The blood will cleanse

41

Goodbye tomorrow
After tomorrow
Hello open sky
Swallow me whole
Tomorrow we die

42

Goodbye, my dying world
My darkening light
My endless night

43

Life cannot be given
In its absence, dignity shall

44

No happy endings
No foregone conclusions

45

We laughed together
We died alone

46

The moon danced
The stars sang
Together they wrote tomorrow

47

Blackness all around
Forward through an endless black tunnel
Oh such a lack of light!
Light that cannot be found
Other than by other light
Light found only by light is no light at all

48

Memory born
Only to die

49

Wrapped in metal
Bound by flesh
Held by programmed desires
No one to hold
I am left alone

50

Memory fades
The heart still beats

51

For her, it beats forever and more

52

I have become perfectly undone

ONE LAZY SUNDAY IN LA A GIRL WALKED INTO A PIZZA SHOP

53

> *Alone I drink from an empty cup*
> *Together there is a future where we do not*
> > *thirst*
> *Now get up!*
> *We have risen!*

JOSIAH GOLOJUH

ONE LAZY SUNDAY IN LA A GIRL WALKED INTO A PIZZA SHOP

PENELOPE THANH-THÙY

December 19, 2024

Penny also has a contribution to this book as she has had to our lives. The impact of our daughters has been immeasurable. The challenge to get anything done is immense, but so it the inspiration to do *everything* for them.

Penny came up with very elaborate plan to write her contribution in secret. Here and there and she had assistance from her friend Harmony. She suggested the opening line. Penny said, "I know Mom doesn't like Nutella, but I do so I'll put that in there."

MOM
Roses are red violets are blue
Mommy I love you
Also Daddy too
You are sweeter than Nutella Mom!
I love love you Mom
And Primy too
She loves you too

JOSIAH GOLOJUH

ONE LAZY SUNDAY IN LA A GIRL WALKED INTO A PIZZA SHOP

PRIMROSE MAI-THANH

December 19, 2024

Prim can pretty much only write her name, so I'll have to dictate her entry into this volume.

"I will write Primrose," Prim said. "Then you will write I like Mommy and then that's it."

Then she was quiet for a bit, well not quiet, just not talking about her poem for Mommy.

Then suddenly, she said "Dad can you write mommy I love you? Then I will just draw a little heart."

That is the story of Prim's contribution to the book.

MOM
Primrose.
I like Mommy.
Mommy I love you.

JOSIAH GOLOJUH

ONE LAZY SUNDAY IN LA A GIRL WALKED INTO A PIZZA SHOP

STEPS

December 19, 2024

Judy and I have been married 15 years. Time is at once a thief that seems to take those years all so suddenly. However, time is also the gift of process. It is a matter of putting one foot in front of the other. Rankin Bass first taught me that with *Santa Clause is Coming to Town*.

A young Chris Kringle, not quite yet even Santa (and voiced by Mickey Rooney), is confronted by the Snow Miser. The Snow Miser doesn't know how to change. He is bad and does not know how to be good. Chris tells him it is a process. You do it one step at a time, like learning to walk you put one foot in front of the other.

I do my best, for Judy, for Penny, for Prim, to be good. To put one foot in front of the other.

If I have know you and hurt you, I am sorry.

If I don't know you and someone you love has hurt you. I am sorry.

I pray that you are able to heal.

I pray they are able to heal.

I hope we are all able to put one foot in front of the other and take a few steps forward.

Judy and I have been hurt. Deeply, we do our best to take those steps. Sometimes it feels like we take one step up and two steps back. There are bruised and broken bones. We stop and rest. We then get to walking, putting one foot in front of the other.

I don't know who, or how many. I assume one person, someone I don't know has made it this far. For you I am grateful. This is primarily for Judy. Yet as I type these words I just feel a strong sense that somewhere out there, some stranger holds this book in their hands. Like Judy and I, you've been hurt, you have the scars, you hold our book of lamentations. Take a step and write you own.

Judy and I had our wedding on December 19th because we absolutely could not wait to start our life together. While our life has by no means been perfect, our love has been tested, the proximity of our anniversary to Christmas acts as a reminder of the things we often forget.

STEPS
Every step
Every struggle
Every tear
Every laugh
Every kiss
Every fight
Every apology
Every success
Every failure
Every joke
Every song
Every dance
Every spider and bug
Every burnt piece of chicken
Every blown fuse
Every guest in our home
Every sleepless night with our daughters
One foot in front of the other
But we must also stop
Wounds heal
Scars need to be allowed to form
Celebrate how far we've come
Because that distance traveled
We have done so together

JOSIAH GOLOJUH

ONE LAZY SUNDAY IN LA A GIRL WALKED INTO A PIZZA SHOP

ONE MORE THING

December 15, 2024

It's Sunday evening. I am finishing the cover. The content is done... or as done as it'll be. I will admit I cheated time so that the moments prior to this come on our fifteenth wedding anniversary, but this, *with this we have found time.*

It is now and we are here together. Perhaps, other people are reading this. I hope that they are, but I am writing this for you, Judy.

Remember.

We found each other just as we needed to. That is why the book has the title, because that is when time began. There are poems in the volume that come prior to you walking through that pizza shop door (Enzo's in Westwood for the record). However, the gift that walked with you Judy was your grace and courage.

Over the years in both of us those things have been chiseled away by circumstance, but I remember. I remember how I felt when I first saw you. Not because I need to recall, but no matter how crushed life and people make me feel, you make me feel love.

Remember.
Remember.
Remember.

A girl walked into a pizza shop and she smiled at me. She gave me love, she gave me courage, and I am giving her and anyone else who wants to read it a book of poetry.

Because Dr. Octopus kind of suggested doing that in *Spider-Man 2*.

ONE LAZY SUNDAY IN LA A GIRL WALKED INTO A PIZZA SHOP

A NOTE FROM JOSIAH

Thank you for reading this experimental work. It is first a gift to Judy and a final thank you to Coleman Hough for always challenging me to go beyond just "telling stories the same way." If you made it this far please leave a review on Amazon and Goodreads and share about this book.

With that I am a storyteller. Find my other stories, *The Paper Boy* featured on the next page, with more to come. This includes a revised and updated version of my short story book with new stories.

Again, thanks. Find my other work. It's better than this but the passion is equal in all my work.

A final note within this note: this version was edited by Judy.

JOSIAH GOLOJUH

THE PAPER BOY NOW AVAILABLE

Daniel's paper route is his refuge from the harsh realities of growing up. Navigating a neighborhood filled with unique and often troubling characters, he seeks solace in his imagination.

When Daniel discovers the body of a young boy hanging from a tree, his world is shaken. Haunted by the ghost, he forms an unlikely bond, teaching his new friend about superheroes and sci-fi. But the truth about the Corpse Boy's death leads Daniel to a sinister revelation involving Cowboy, a dangerous figure from the trailer park.

As a storm brews, Daniel must confront his deepest fears and face a chilling showdown with Cowboy. In a neighborhood on the brink of chaos, Daniel's courage will be tested in ways he never imagined.

"The Paper Boy" is a gripping tale of friendship, loss, and the dark secrets that lurk beneath the surface.

Find it online at Amazon and Barnes & Noble.

ONE LAZY SUNDAY IN LA A GIRL WALKED INTO A PIZZA SHOP

THE PAPER BOY NOW AVAILABLE

"The best .... book you will read, funny, dark, referential and clever, Josiah isn't clowning around."
Stephen Chiodo writer/director, Killer Klowns from Outer Space

"Scary, intriguing and exciting ... The ... Pennsylvania setting lends itself perfectly to the movie that will soon be following .... we hope!"
Dawn Keezer - Director, Pittsburgh Film Office

"*The Paper Boy* is a clever and suspenseful contribution to the superhero genre. Josiah Golojuh will keep you guessing and make you think at the same time."
Tom Perrotta - Oscar Nominated Writer, *Little Children*, *Election*, *The Leftovers*

"There's a reason Josiah Golojuh calls his YouTube channel, Josiah is Write - this fella can really write!"
Stephen Stern - Co-Creator, Zen: Intergalactic Ninja

JOSIAH GOLOJUH

YOUNG ZOMBIE NOW AVAILABLE

Meta fiction from the world of The Paper Boy. Find out the origin story of the Young Zombie in, *Young Zombie: Tales From The R.I.P. - Deluxe Edition*. Digital only.

An unbelievable 80 Pages of content! Undead and unbeatable value!

- The **20**-page *Young Zombie* story!
- The full project history, including the previously lost original short film script!
- **25 *Tales from the Crypt*-style** comic pages, from the rare anthology *Astounding Tales of Adventure* featuring the original **6-page** version of *Young Zombie* (then known as *I Was a Teenage Zombie*).
- Character design and model sheets!
- Cover gallery featuring art by **Bill Maus** and 6-year-old **Penny Golojuh**!

available at

ONE LAZY SUNDAY IN LA A GIRL WALKED INTO A PIZZA SHOP

SUBSCRIBE TO JOSIAH IS WRITE

Geek Culture Explained on **YouTube**. Where you can watch the feature length documentary *Zen: Intergalactic Ninja - The Complete History* written and directed by **Josiah Golojuh** featuring interviews with co-creators **Steve Stern** & **Dan Cote**, artist/writer, **Bill Maus**, Entity Comics publisher **Don Chin** and more!

COMING SOON TO KICKSTARTER

The Borough is coming to Kickstarter! More metafiction from *The Paper Boy* is coming in 2025. Meet characters referenced in *The Paper Boy* in their ideal comic book form, including The Illuminator, Hero, Hero II, Merkanary, and of course **The Grim & The Ghoul**! Help us bring these Main Title characters to life in 2025 and beyond with these "lost" 90s comics!

JOSIAH GOLOJUH

www.ingramcontent.com/pod-product-compliance
Lightning Source LLC
Chambersburg PA
CBHW051653040426
42446CB00009B/1113